U.S. Department of Justice
Office of Justice Programs
National Institute of Justice

 I0448560

NATIONAL INSTITUTE OF JUSTICE

ANNUAL REPORT

2012

U.S. Department of Justice
Office of Justice Programs
810 Seventh St. N.W.
Washington, DC 20531

Eric H. Holder, Jr.
Attorney General

Karol V. Mason
Assistant Attorney General

Greg Ridgeway
Acting Director, National Institute of Justice

This and other publications and products of the
National Institute of Justice can be found at:

National Institute of Justice
http://www.nij.gov

Office of Justice Programs
Innovation • Partnerships • Safer Neighborhoods

To the President, the Attorney General and the Congress:

It is my honor to transmit the National Institute of Justice's annual report on research, development and evaluation for fiscal year 2012, pursuant to Title 1 of the Omnibus Crime Control and Safe Streets Act of 1968 and Title II of the Homeland Security Act of 2002.

Respectfully submitted,

Gregory K. Ridgeway, Ph.D.
Acting Director, National Institute of Justice

Table of Contents

Overview   3

NIJ's Strategic Challenges 2012   4

Fostering Science-Based Criminal Justice Practice   5

Translating Knowledge to Practice   8

Advancing Technology   12

Working Across Disciplines   15

Adopting a Global Perspective   17

Highlights of Dissemination   19

Highlights of Newly Funded Projects in FY 2012   21

Financial Data   24

OVERVIEW

The National Institute of Justice is the only federal agency devoted solely to bringing the benefits of scientific research and technology development to the nation's criminal justice system. We are the research and development arm of the U.S. Department of Justice. Our mission is to help criminal justice professionals by conducting research, assessing new technologies, promoting innovations and evaluating programs to learn what works and what does not work. NIJ applies a rigorous approach in all its efforts, both for those that benefit the larger criminal justice community and those that strengthen the internal workings of the Institute.

In fiscal year 2012, NIJ moved to strengthen its peer review process. The Institute launched a pilot effort to use standing panels and used the new Standing Scientific Review Panels to evaluate and score applications from 11 of NIJ's 39 solicitations. (The remaining 28 solicitations were reviewed using NIJ's traditional scientific review panels.) The Standing Scientific Review Panels are larger than NIJ's traditional panels. Thus, they provide greater quality and breadth to the review process. Based on preliminary assessments, NIJ has decided to use the new Standing Scientific Review Panels again in fiscal year 2013.

The Institute works closely with criminal justice professionals to set its research priorities. We sponsor and attend topic-centered meetings, roundtables, and working groups to listen and obtain ideas for our research agendas. To strengthen our ability to work collaboratively, NIJ created a new office in 2012. The new Office of Research Partnerships cultivates relationships inside and outside government to build on NIJ's strengths.

The following pages provide just a sampling of the most prominent work undertaken by NIJ, where researchers harness the power of science to make the American justice system more effective and equitable.

The Institute disseminates research findings through various formats, including print, online, multimedia, and in-person gatherings. See "Highlights of 2012 Dissemination Activity" for examples. Visit NIJ.gov for further details on the topics and projects discussed in this annual report.

NIJ'S STRATEGIC CHALLENGES 2012

NIJ is committed to transforming the criminal justice field by meeting these challenges:

1. **FOSTERING SCIENCE-BASED CRIMINAL JUSTICE PRACTICE:** Supporting scientific research to ensure the safety of families, schools and communities.

2. **TRANSLATING KNOWLEDGE TO PRACTICE:** Disseminating scientific research to criminal justice professionals to advance what works best in crime prevention and reduction.

3. **ADVANCING TECHNOLOGY:** Building a more efficient, effective and fair criminal justice system.

4. **WORKING ACROSS DISCIPLINES:** Drawing on physical, forensic and social sciences to reduce crime and promote justice.

5. **ADOPTING A GLOBAL PERSPECTIVE:** Understanding crime rates and their social contexts at home and abroad.

CHAPTER 1

FOSTERING SCIENCE-BASED CRIMINAL JUSTICE PRACTICE

NIJ's fostering of science-based practices follows three integrated steps:

1. Develop new findings, tools and technologies.
2. Translate, transfer and communicate to the field.
3. Test and evaluate how well the new ideas, tools and technologies work in the field.

Strengthening the Forensic Sciences

To strengthen the fundamental underpinnings of forensic science disciplines, NIJ funds some of the most internationally renowned agencies, universities and institutions in the U.S., and all of NIJ's forensic R&D partners — both inside and outside of academia — are culturally rooted in scientific development. In fact, historically, the number of awards in NIJ's forensic R&D portfolio exceeds that of any other federal agency.

NIJ's forensics portfolio includes studies about physical, life and cognitive sciences and focuses on:

- The strengths and limits of analytical procedures.
- Sources of bias and variation.
- Quantification of uncertainties created by these sources.
- Measures of performance.
- Procedural steps in analyzing forensic evidence.
- Methods to oversee and improve steps in forensic evidence analysis.

Advancing and Transferring DNA Technology to the Field

NIJ has become a global leader in integrating DNA technology into the criminal justice system. The Institute funds research and development to produce faster, cheaper and more effective DNA tests and funds the Forensic Science Center of Excellence to evaluate new technologies and promote technology transfer to crime labs.

In FY 2012, NIJ received $117 million in appropriations for DNA and other forensic programs. Of this total, close to $105 million was available for use on grants and contracts. About 81 percent went directly to, or benefited, crime laboratories to reduce their backlog of

NIJ

DNA samples and increase laboratory capacity. Funds also went to police departments to identify missing persons and solve cold cases. About 13 percent went to DNA and other forensics research and development. Another 6 percent was used for training and technical assistance to increase the use of DNA and other forensics in the criminal justice system.

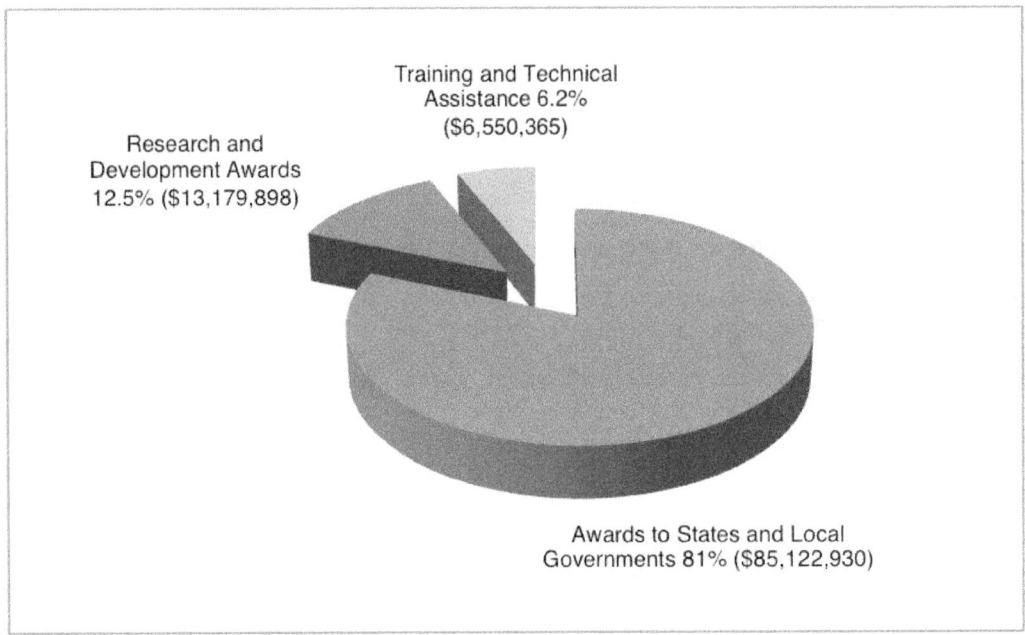

Figure 1. Allocation of DNA Initiative Funds

Scientific advances have allowed analysts to test ever smaller-sized samples and samples that have been badly degraded. Such advances help investigators solve crimes, but they are also helping crime labs find new ways to expand their capacity and process cases more quickly. NIJ funding helps labs to modernize equipment, train analysts to use it, adopt more efficient management strategies and hire additional analysts.

Advances in technology are also making it possible to analyze unidentified human remains and family reference samples to support efforts to identify missing persons. Investigators can also solve more cold cases by applying DNA testing to previously unsolved crimes.

To carry the benefits of new scientific discoveries to the field, NIJ supports training programs that give crime lab analysts opportunities to learn to use newly developed techniques and technologies. The Institute also supports activities through which analysts can share findings. In fiscal year 2012, for example, NIJ published *Law 101: Legal Guide for the Forensic Expert,* which has become one of NIJ's most popular online training courses. The Institute also published the third in a series of educational materials about using DNA in the courtroom: *DNA for the Defense Bar* joined the *Principles of Forensic DNA for Officers of the Court, DNA: A Prosecutor's Notebook* and *DNA for Law*

Enforcement Decision Makers in explaining how DNA can be used to defend the innocent and convict the guilty.

▶ **Learn more** on NIJ.gov, keyword "DNA Initiative report to Congress."

Untangling Issues About Sexual Assault

NIJ is working with several jurisdictions to understand why sexual assault kits go untested and what can be done to eliminate backlogs of untested kits in the future. The goal is to move beyond the "crisis management of the moment" to the adoption of systematic practices, procedures and protocols that bring together multidisciplinary teams of researchers and representatives from the police departments, crime labs, prosecutor's offices and community-based victim services organizations.

Houston, Texas, and Wayne County, Mich., are exploring why so many sexual assault kits are not forwarded from police evidence rooms to crime labs. While the researchers are uncovering why, the labs are also testing many previously untested kits.

▶ **Learn more** on NIJ.gov, keyword "untested sexual assault."

Improving Sexual Assault Exams

NIJ teamed up with the Office for Victims of Crime to study sexual assault medical forensic examinations. A forum of experts explored gaps in the existing research related to the technical aspects of sexual assault medical forensic examinations. The goal was to identify what research is needed to bring a stronger evidence base to these examinations. The forum focused on the following topics:

- Types of evidence gathered.
- Examination technology.
- Standardizing the evidence kit.
- Evolving DNA technology.
- Potential use and logistics of telemedicine during the examination.

▶ **Learn more** on NIJ.gov, keyword "sexual assault medical forensic exam."

Numerous studies suggest that Sexual Assault Nurse Examiners (SANEs) are helpful to police and prosecutors and that the evidence they collect is more likely to result in arrest and prosecution. In 2009, NIJ funded development of a toolkit for evaluating the impact of SANEs. The toolkit outlines, step by step, what communities can do to validate the effectiveness of a newly installed SANE program. Following the development of the toolkit, NIJ funded researchers to assess the impact of the toolkit across multiple sites.

▶ **See** a number of products related to the SANE toolkit on NCJRS.gov, keyword "SANE toolkit."

CHAPTER 2

TRANSLATING KNOWLEDGE TO PRACTICE

NIJ emphasizes useful research that can be quickly adopted by people who work in the criminal justice system. Translational criminology aims to break down barriers between basic and applied research by creating a dynamic interface between research and practice. The process is a two-way street: Scientists discover new tools and ideas for use in the field and evaluate their impact; in turn, practitioners offer novel observations from the field.

Testing HOPE on the American Mainland

NIJ launched an effort to replicate and evaluate a promising, innovative probation program in four new sites. The four sites will replicate Hawaii's Opportunity Probation with Enforcement (HOPE). Hawaii's program identifies probationers at high risk of violating the terms of their community supervision and imposes frequent and random supervision conditions, such as drug testing and swift, certain jail stays for violations. The program also provides treatment when necessary. An NIJ-funded evaluation of Hawaii's drug-involved offenders in HOPE found that combining random drug tests and swift and certain sanctions for probation violations showed great promise. When compared to offenders who received conventional probation, after one year the HOPE probationers were 72 percent less likely to use drugs. They were also 55 percent less likely to be arrested for a new crime, 61 percent less likely to skip appointments with their probation officers and 53 percent less likely to have their probation revoked.

NIJ and the Bureau of Justice Assistance collaborated to begin testing the Hawaii model in four new sites: Saline County, Ark.; Tarrant County, Texas; Essex County, Mass. and Clackamas County, Ore. All four sites have agreed to replicate the Hawaii model so evaluators can find out whether the effort can be successfully reproduced outside Hawaii. BJA is managing the demonstration sites and NIJ is managing the evaluations.

Meanwhile, researchers at Pepperdine University are evaluating the long-term impact of the original HOPE program. They had previously found dramatic reductions in missed probation appointments, positive drug tests and arrests for new offenses. The researchers are looking at the original groups to see whether, after five years had passed, the HOPE probationers still performed better than those who had conventional probation.

▶ **Learn more** on NIJ.gov, keyword: "Hawaii HOPE."

NIJ

Longer Shifts Work Better for Law Enforcement

Police executives can improve morale and reduce overtime by instituting 10-hour shifts. Researchers conducted a randomized controlled experiment in two police departments comparing eight-, 10- and 12-hour days. The results revealed no significant differences between the three shift lengths on work performance, health or work–family conflict. Officers working 10-hour shifts reported significantly higher quality of work life than those on eight-hour shifts. They also worked fewer overtime hours. The NIJ-funded study was conducted by the Police Foundation.

▶ **Learn more** on NIJ.gov, keyword "police fatigue."

Research on Wrongful Convictions

NIJ has a robust portfolio of awards to states to examine cases where testing of DNA evidence may prove the innocence of previously convicted people.

In 2012, an NIJ-funded study took a close look at one state to determine the number of wrongful convictions. An Urban Institute team examined 634 homicide and sexual assault cases that occurred in Virginia between 1973 and 1987 where physical evidence was retained. The researchers found that in 33 of the sexual assault convictions (8 percent of the total in the study), DNA testing ruled-out the person who was convicted and supported exoneration.

▶ **Read the full report,** *Post-Conviction DNA Testing and Wrongful Conviction,* at https://www.ncjrs.gov/pdffiles1/nij/grants/238816.pdf.

NIJ teamed up with the International Association of Chiefs of Police to host a summit on wrongful convictions in August 2012. The summit participants discussed problems and possible solutions in four broad areas: wrongful arrests, wrongful convictions, forensic and investigative technology, and exonerations. The summit included police, prosecutors, defense attorneys and judges.

Research on Prosecution and Defense

NIJ sponsored research by the Vera Institute of Justice on prosecutorial case-screening decisions, charging decisions, plea offers, sentence recommendations and dismissals in two county prosecutors' offices. The researchers found that objective strength of evidence was the determining factor in most screening decisions. After that, contextual factors such as offense severity, criminal history and victim characteristics were considered. All decisions were constrained by office policies, resources and working relationships with judges and other agencies.

University of Maryland researchers recently combined federal arrest and court disposition data to gain insights into why prosecutors tend to decline cases or negotiate charge reductions. Weak evidence was the most often-cited reason for declining a case. The offender's sex was sometimes a factor, with females receiving charge reductions.

Researchers at the RAND Corp. reviewed murder cases in Philadelphia. They found that public defenders reduce their clients' murder conviction rate by 19 percent, lower the chance that their clients receive a life sentence by 62 percent and reduce expected time served in prison by 24 percent compared to appointed counsel. Judges and attorneys identified fee structures and other institutional factors as possible explanations for why appointed counsel may not prepare cases as well as the Defender Association attorneys.

NIJ is also sponsoring several other research projects on indigent defense, including an assessment of the state of indigent defense services for mentally ill defendants.

Reentry of Former Prisoners

The Second Chance Act is designed to increase reentry programming for offenders returning to their families and communities. NIJ is funding a number of evaluations to see whether the new programming is reducing recidivism, including:

- An evaluation of reentry courts.
- Two evaluations of the impact of programming on medium-to-high-risk adult offenders.
- An evaluation of juvenile reentry demonstration projects.
- A multisite demonstration field experiment that will examine the implementation of a promising reentry intervention.

Each project is using rigorous methods to assess the impact of programs and compare the costs of developing and implementing Second Chance Act reentry services to traditional programming. Results of the evaluations will be available in several years.

▶ **See the awards** related to evaluating the Second Chance Act on NIJ.gov, keyword "Second Chance."

▶ **See all NIJ awards** on NIJ.gov, keyword "list of awards."

Reentry Program for Violent Offenders Had Mixed Results

Researchers followed up on participants in the Serious and Violent Offender Reentry Initiative program. More than 2,300 participants, including adults of both sexes and juvenile males, were in either a test program or a comparison group between 2004 and 2007. Researchers augmented the original data with additional years of post-release arrest and incarceration data. Participation in the test programs was associated with longer times to arrest and fewer arrests for all three demographic groups during a minimum follow-up period of 56 months for the adults and 22 months for the juveniles. The researchers found differences in outcomes depending on the types of services offered. Services oriented toward practical needs, including reentry preparation, life skills programs and employment services did not improve post-release non-recidivism results for men, including housing, employment and drug use results. Sometimes these services interfered with successful reintegration.

▶ **Read the full report,** *Prisoner Reentry Services: What Worked for SVORI Evaluation Participants?* at https://www.ncjrs.gov/pdffiles1/nij/grants/238214.pdf.

CHAPTER 3

ADVANCING TECHNOLOGY

NIJ has been at the forefront of efforts to make law enforcement more efficient through the wise use of technological innovations. The Institute works closely with law enforcement and corrections agencies to develop standards and adopt new technologies in a cost-effective manner.

NIJ Issues Bomb Suit Standard

The Institute published its first bomb suit standard in March 2012. The performance standard applies to suits worn by bomb technicians when they work to disarm or dispose of an explosive device. The standard is the fruit of years of work with bomb squad commanders, researchers and manufacturers. It defines both performance requirements and the methods used to test performance.

▶ **Learn more** on NIJ.gov, keyword "bomb suit standard."

Sex Offenders Tracked by GPS Commit Fewer Crimes

A large study of California high-risk sex offenders on parole found that those who were placed on GPS monitoring had significantly lower recidivism rates than a control group that received traditional supervision. The study involved just over 500 people. A cost analysis showed that the GPS program is more expensive but more effective than traditional supervision. Monitoring parolees using GPS costs $35.96 a day per person, while the cost of traditional supervision is about $27.45 a day. The GPS program costs $8.51 more per day, but produced a 12 percentage-point decrease in arrests (from 26.36 percent to 14.34 percent).

▶ **Read the press release** at
http://www.ojp.usdoj.gov/newsroom/pressreleases/2012/ojppr051012.pdf.

▶ **Read the full report,** *Monitoring High-Risk Sex Offenders with GPS Technology: An Evaluation of the California Supervision Program,* at
https://www.ncjrs.gov/pdffiles1/nij/grants/238481.pdf.

NIJ

Challenge to Scientists and Engineers to Assess the Service Life of Body Armor

Body armor, popularly known as bulletproof vests, has saved the lives of more than 3,000 law enforcement officers. This critical piece of safety equipment is usually warranted to last for three to five years. NIJ issued a challenge that includes a $50,000 cash award for creative ways to learn when an officer's vest needs to be replaced. Firing a bullet at a vest is one quick way to find out how it is holding up, but does so much damage that the vest cannot be safely used after that. NIJ is calling for non-destructive ways to assess the service life of vests.

▶ **Learn more** on NIJ.gov, keyword: "body armor challenge."

Telemedicine Center for Sexual Assault Victims

NIJ teamed up with the Justice Department's Office for Victims of Crime to begin funding a sexual assault forensic medical examination telemedicine center. Research has shown that SANE programs and Sexual Assault Response Teams (SART) improve health care quality for sexual assault victims, improve the quality of forensic evidence collected and result in increased prosecution rates over time. Several states are using telemedicine to deliver sexual assault forensic exams to children in rural or tribal areas. This program would make such services available to adults. It will involve setting up a national telemedicine center for sexual assault medical examinations, using four pilot sites and testing the pilot programs' viability. The pilot programs will provide 24-7 live assistance by trained SANEs. There will be one of each of the following types of sites: military, rural, tribal and correctional. The Massachusetts Department of Public Safety will set up the center.

▶ **Learn more** on OVC.gov, keyword "telemedicine."

Recovery of Burned Human Remains

This study addressed the multiple forensic aspects of the recovery and interpretation of burned human remains. It linked rigorous scene recovery and documentation methods with laboratory analyses of heat-altered human remains from fatal fire scenes. This research showed that a fatal fire scene could be completely excavated in a few days. This can be done with comprehensive documentation, high evidence detection and recovery rates, and minimal evidence change. A complex fire scene can be processed and documented in two to three days. The evidence recovery exercises showed that evidence could still be detected, identified and analyzed after aggressive fire-suppression efforts. Further, the study showed that regular, clear, normal patterns of heat alteration of the human body can be identified and successfully used to detect suspicious cases.

▶ **Read the full report,** *Recovery and Interpretation of Burned Human Remains,* at
https://www.ncjrs.gov/pdffiles1/nij/grants/237966.pdf.

Developing an Offender Tracking System Standard

NIJ is working with corrections professionals and manufacturers to develop the first voluntary, minimum performance standards and testing protocols for offender-tracking technologies (including GPS, cellular technology and monitoring center equipment). The work involves a review of existing standards and test methods that could be adopted for the testing of electronic monitoring equipment. Many state and local agencies use tracking technologies as an aid in supervising people who are on probation or parole, but the many devices on the market vary considerably. A national standard will help officials make wiser purchasing decisions knowing that products that meet the NIJ standards will return reliable location information regardless of the conditions under which they are used.

▶ **Learn more** on NIJ.gov, keyword "offender tracking."

WORKING ACROSS DISCIPLINES

NIJ has a long history of working with like-minded organizations, ranging from the MacArthur Foundation to the Centers for Disease Control and Prevention. These partnerships have provided unique opportunities to cross-fertilize the knowledge NIJ builds. They also forge stronger relationships with others who share our goals. See the Overview for discussion of NIJ's Office of Research Partnerships and its role in strengthening NIJ's effort to work across disciplines.

Looking for Connections Between Crime and Traffic

NIJ teamed up with the National Highway Traffic Safety Administration to examine the relationship between crime rates and traffic incidents. Anecdotal evidence suggests that crime rates often move in tandem with traffic violations. Six localities around the country are taking part in a pilot project to identify places where crime and traffic accident hot spots overlap. Local police departments will then test high visibility enforcement strategies to see what impact they have on crime and traffic accident rates. This research builds on previous work that indicates a focus by police on crime hot spots has a positive effect. NIJ is assessing the feasibility of conducting an evaluation of the programs using rigorous research methods.

▶ **Learn more** on NIJ.gov, keyword "crime and traffic."

Roadside Safety

NIJ worked with the U.S. Fire Administration to find the best ways to make vehicles more visible on the road, keeping public safety officers safer. The teams have confirmed a number of techniques for improving patrol car visibility:

- Higher intensity warning lights are more effective during the day but have no effect at night.
- Blue lights are the easiest light color for the driving public to see.
- Reflective materials should be placed lower on emergency vehicles to take advantage of headlights from approaching vehicles.

NIJ

Researchers are continuing to explore other tools and techniques to improve visibility. These include testing the effectiveness of the pattern of striping on vehicles and the use of highway flares and reflective vests.

▶ **Learn more** on NIJ.gov, keyword "roadside safety."

Geospatial Technology Tested in Lincoln, Neb.

The Lincoln Police Department and researchers at the University of Nebraska are collaborating on a project to test and evaluate location-aware mobile applications for proactive community policing. The services provide locations of known persons of interest, officer locations and situational awareness data. Using the same technology that powers location-based searching for restaurants, officers can receive locations of people of interest such as those who have outstanding warrants, gang members, parolees and registered sex offenders. Officers can also see where other officers are. In the first six months of use, the system was credited with helping officers to make an additional 177 arrests.

Improving a Decision-Making Tool

RTI International developed a software tool that helps agencies analyze 911 calls to identify areas at elevated risk for criminal activity in the near future. This tool enables the identification of calls that imply an immediate risk for responding officers.

Creating Computer Models for Predictive Policing

NIJ continues to invest in research and development for tools and techniques that can help law enforcement understand risk factors for new crimes and forecast where crime might occur. Predictive policing creates models that show crime trends over long periods as well as short-term changes.

CHAPTER 5

ADOPTING A GLOBAL PERSPECTIVE

As modern air travel and electronic communications extend criminal activities beyond national borders, research about international crimes (such as terrorism, organized crime, trafficking in persons and cybercrime) require partnerships with government and nongovernment agencies. These partnerships help state and local entities in the U.S. to understand the impact of international crime on our communities.

Launching New International Initiatives

NIJ signed an official agreement with the Netherlands Forensic Institute and the Netherlands Organization for Scientific Research to collaborate on projects designed to improve the criminal justice systems in both countries. The Institute also launched a new partnership with the Australia New Zealand Policing Advisory Agency to collaborate in new research and development projects and to evaluate new forensic technologies in the field. These agreements, or memoranda of understanding (MOU), establish a framework for the partners to leverage areas of mutual interest.

Meanwhile, NIJ launched a new collaboration with the United Kingdom's Home Office that involves joint research on organized crime.

▶ **Learn more** on NIJ.gov, keyword "MOU."

Human Trafficking

Two studies by NIJ illuminate the world of human trafficking to find ways to prevent the problem and successfully prosecute cases that do occur.

The first study resulted in the launch of a comprehensive, interactive online listing of more than 875 cities and counties that have used a variety of tactics to deter men from buying sex. The researchers categorize and describe 12 major types of tactics. In their final report, they note that the evidence is slowly accumulating about which demand-reduction tactics (and comprehensive approaches that include reducing demand) can effectively suppress commercial sex markets. Effective demand-reduction efforts range from "john schools" for those who solicit prostitutes to seizing automobiles and using surveillance cameras in anti-prostitution efforts.

▶ **Visit** www.DemandForum.org.

▶ **Read the full report,** *A National Overview of Prostitution and Sex Trafficking Demand Reduction Efforts,* at https://www.ncjrs.gov/pdffiles1/nij/grants/238796.pdf.

The second study examined why few trafficking cases are prosecuted at the state and local level. Researchers looked at 15 counties across the U.S. They found that most trafficking cases begin with a tip from someone who knows about the situation, but rarely from trafficked people themselves. Researchers found that 69 percent of the reviewed cases went forward to prosecution, but most offenders were not charged with trafficking. Instead, they were prosecuted under older laws, such as those against promoting prostitution. Local prosecutors sometimes lacked the resources to travel and collect evidence when cases would span county or state lines, as trafficking organizations often do. In addition, local prosecutors tend to regard such cases as a federal matter.

▶ **Read the full report,** *Identifying Challenges to Improve the Investigation and Prosecution of State and Local Human Trafficking Cases,* at https://www.ncjrs.gov/pdffiles1/nij/grants/238795.pdf.

Work With the Peace Corps

NIJ provided technical assistance at the request of the U.S. Peace Corps to help the agency design an effective crime victimization survey of volunteers. This action followed passage of the Kate Puzey Peace Corps Volunteer Protection Act. The goal was to share NIJ's research expertise about the best practices for implementing and evaluating the results of a survey the Peace Corps must implement as a result of the act.

NIJ

Chapter 6

HIGHLIGHTS OF DISSEMINATION

Research for the Real World Seminars

NIJ's in-person seminar series is held periodically in Washington, D.C., and features research that is changing our thinking about policies and practices. The seminars are recorded before a live audience and posted on NIJ.gov.

▶ **Learn more** on NIJ.gov, keyword "research for the real world."

Research Digest

NIJ publishes its research results throughout the year on NIJ.gov. Final reports are archived on NCJRS.gov. NIJ also publishes short summaries of recent results in the quarterly Research Report Digest.

▶ **Find it** on NIJ.gov, keyword "digest."

Protecting Protectors

NIJ summarized major findings from the portfolio of research on officer safety in a brochure that was distributed at major events and locations during Police Week in April 2012. Subsequently, the brochure has been reprinted and distributed in a number of ways, including by an insurance company that insures public safety officers in Virginia.

▶ **Read or download** the brochure on NCJRS.gov, keyword "protecting protectors."

Outside Publications

NIJ shares research findings in a variety of association publications. In 2012, NIJ staffers contributed to publications ranging from the American Academy of Forensic Sciences newsletter to *Corrections Today.*

DNA for the Defense Bar

NIJ published a guide for defense attorneys about how to take advantage of DNA testing technology. It joins related products that explain the science of DNA testing and includes a discussion of the statistics used in DNA analysis. The document has been extremely popular. The New York Defense Bar, for example, requested 135 copies to be distributed at every public defender's office in the state.

▶ **Read or download** the guide at https://www.ncjrs.gov/pdffiles1/nij/237975.pdf.

Law 101: Legal Guide for the Forensic Expert

One of NIJ's newest online trainings has become one of its most popular. *Law 101* discusses recommended practices for forensic experts who must prepare for and testify in court.

▶ **Take the class** on NIJ.gov, keyword: "Law 101 training."

Chapter 7

HIGHLIGHTS OF NEWLY FUNDED PROJECTS IN FY 2012

Each year, NIJ issues solicitations for research and formula grants programs (such as the Coverdell Forensic Science Improvement Grants Program). The application process is highly competitive. Proposals received under a solicitation are reviewed by independent peer panels comprising reviewers from academia, industry, and government organizations, along with practitioners from federal, state, and local agencies. Once reviewers have completed evaluations, NIJ program managers recommend individual proposals to the NIJ Director, who makes final award decisions.

The complete list of awards can be found on NIJ.gov, keyword "list of awards," and contains the solicitation, the number of applications received and the awards made, the value of awards and an abstract of each award. Highlights are below:

Victims

Case Attrition in Sexual Assault Cases

This project will determine the factors that contribute to sexual assault cases not moving forward in the criminal justice system; that is, why there are not more cases that lead to charges or prosecutions. Researchers at the University of Massachusetts will examine cases in at least six jurisdictions.

Effects of Child Maltreatment

University of Washington researchers will look at the long-term effects of child maltreatment. Specifically, they will follow up with a group of 457 people who either had contact with child welfare workers in 1976 and 1977 or were members of a control group. (The children were preschool-age at the time). The study will examine possible long-term effects of maltreatment related to substance abuse, mental health status and antisocial behavior.

Offenders

Violent Extremism in the U.S.

NIJ launched a program to study domestic radicalization, with an emphasis on learning how people move into the realm of violent extremism. The research will focus on understanding extremism and advancing strategies for effective prevention and intervention. These studies will look at group dynamics as well as "lone wolf" terrorists. The research will also evaluate community-level programs that have shown promise in preventing or countering violent radicalization in the U.S. NIJ made six research contracts and one evaluation award for a total of $3.2 million.

Forensics

Paper Microfluidic Systems

Researchers at Florida International University will work to develop and validate a paper microfluidic device that can detect explosives. Paper microfluidics is a new technology that permits the development of inexpensive systems that can be used in on-site forensic testing.

Bath Salts Detection

"Bath salts" are illegal drugs derived from the khat shrub native to Africa and Arabia. They are increasingly popular among American recreational drug users. Researchers at Sam Houston State University will work on developing new analytical methods that can accurately identify at least eight of the most popular drugs.

Policing

Understanding Crime Trends in America

This multidisciplinary roundtable of 14 experts will study factors responsible for the recent 20-year drop in both violent and property crime rates. The roundtable will be a neutral venue for untangling competing explanations for the crime rate decline. NIJ awarded $720,000 to the National Research Council at the National Academy of Sciences for 36 months.

Testing Procedural Justice in Seattle

NIJ will evaluate a training program that promotes the use of procedural justice in the Seattle Police Department. The study will develop a high-risk circumstance model to identify officers working in behavioral hot spots, small geographic areas where officers are more like to be involved in problematic encounters with citizens. Officers will be randomly assigned to control and experimental groups. The impact of procedural justice training will be measured by various outcomes such as officer safety, use of force, citizen complaints, the number and composition of arrests made by officers, and the use of warnings and citations as alternatives to arrests.

Understanding the Impact of Technology on Policing

Technologies ranging from radios to conducted energy devices have reshaped law enforcement over the years, but little research exists on the overall impact of new technologies on the field. NIJ is taking a three-pronged approach to this topic:

- The Institute will convene an expert panel to discuss and prioritize the importance of several technologies.
- A nationally representative survey will identify the use and impact of various technologies in law enforcement agencies.
- An evaluation will assess 10 agencies that are "high-technology implementers" and 10 that are low implementers to learn what occurs in the absence of particular technologies and the impact of technology over time on measures such as crime rates and calls for service.

Corrections

Community Corrections Executive Sessions

An Executive Session convenes individuals of independent standing who are prepared to take joint responsibility for rethinking and improving society's responses to an issue over two to four years. The members might be thought of as the Board of Directors, if there were one, for the issue. Harvard University's Kennedy School of Government has refined the concept and process of Executive Sessions over the last 25 years. The fiscal imperative to reduce prison costs and find alternatives was the impetus to launch an Executive Session on community corrections. NIJ awarded Harvard $993,386 to convene an Executive Session on community corrections through 2016.

National Study of Prison Closings and Alternatives Strategies

This research will examine state correctional financial situations, the strategies states are using as they are forced to curtail spending and the tradeoffs they face. The study will describe the strategies and best practices for ensuring public safety and offender rehabilitation. It will also illustrate the long-term impact on crime, including costs and benefits.

FINANCIAL DATA

Exhibit 1: Funds Made Available Pursuant to P.L. 112-55, FY 2012

Type of Funds	Amount in Millions
1. Research, Evaluation and Development NIJ Base Appropriation*	$40.0
2. State and Local Law Enforcement Assistance	
a. DNA related and Other Forensic Programs and Activities	
1. DNA Analysis and Capacity Enhancement Program and for Other Local, State and Federal Forensic Activities	$117.0
2. Postconviction DNA Testing	$4.0
3. Sexual Assault Forensic Exam Program Grants	$4.0
b. Paul Coverdell Forensic Science Improvement Grants	$12.0
c. Domestic Radicalization Research	$4.0
3. Violence Against Women Prevention and Prosecution Programs a. Analysis and Research on Violence Against Indian Women	$1.0
b. Research and Evaluation of Violence Against Women and Related Issues	$3.0
4. Reimbursements and Transfers from Other Federal Entities (including OJP components)	$10.0
5. Section 215 Set-aside for Research and Statistics	$12.9
6. Carryover from Prior Fiscal Years	$2.5
TOTAL FUNDS	$210.4

* P.L. 112-55 directed NIJ to transfer $5 million to the National Institute of Standards and Technology.

Exhibit 2: Allocation of Funds, FY 2012

Type of activity	Subcategory	Percent
Social Science	Evaluation	4.6%
	Research	12.5%
Science and Technology	Research and Development	2.4%
	Standards Development	0.0%
	Technology Assistance/Test & Evaluation	4.9%
Investigative and Forensic Science	Analysis and Capacity Enhancement*	47.2%
	Research and Development	9.2%
	Training and Technical Assistance	1.6%
	National Missing and Unidentified Persons System (NamUs)	1.3%
Dissemination/Outreach/Program Support		3.7%
Carve-out for Section 215 Set-aside for Research and Statistics		1.3%
OJP Management and Administration (M&A)		7.0%
Direct Transfer to the National Institute of Standards and Technology (NIST) Pursuant to Public Law 112-55		2.4%
Carryover**		1.9%
	TOTAL	100.0%

* Grants to states and units of local government to improve and enhance crime laboratories (including funds for analyses/backlog reduction).

** NIJ received "no-year" funding for these programs in FY 2012 (funds that did not expire at the end of the fiscal year). "Carryover" funds are those that remained unobligated as of the end of the fiscal year. Depending on the provisions of future appropriations legislation, these funds may be subject to statutory rescission.

Exhibit 3: Allocation of Funds for DNA-Related and Other Forensics Programs and Activities, FY 2012

The National Institute of Justice received $125 million in FY 2012 appropriations for DNA-related and other forensic programs and activities, which were used as follows:

DNA Analysis, Capacity Enhancement, and Other Forensic Activities	FY 2012 Funds (in millions)	Prior Year Carryover Funds Available for Programs (in millions)*
Awards that Directly Benefit State and Local Government Efforts to Build Capacity and Reduce Backlogs:		
Forensic DNA Backlog Reduction Program**	$74.3	
Solving Cold Cases with DNA	$7.6	
DNA Technology to Identify the Missing	$3.2	
Postconviction DNA Testing Assistance Program***	$0.1	
Research and Development:		
Research, Development and Evaluation (Applied and Basic)	$13.1	
Strategic Approaches to Sexual Assault Kit (SAK) Evidence: An Action Research Project	$0.2	$0.6
Training and Technical Assistance:		
Training and Technical Assistance (including $2.7 million for the National Missing and Unidentified Persons System (NamUs)	$6.6	
Other:		
Carve-out for Section 215 NIJ/BJS Set-aside for Research, Evaluation and Statistics	$2.3	
Office of Justice Programs Assessment for Management and Administration (M&A)	$9.5	
Carryover****	$0.1	
SUBTOTAL	$117.0	$0.6

Postconviction DNA Testing Program	FY 2012 Funds (in millions)	Prior Year Carryover Funds Available for Programs (in millions)*
Postconviction DNA Testing Assistance Program Grants	$3.6	
Office of Justice Programs Assessment for Management and Administration (M&A)	$0.3	
Peer Review of Postconviction Applications	$0.1	
Carryover****	$0.0	
SUBTOTAL	$4.0	$0.0

Sexual Assault Forensic Exam Program	FY 2012 Funds (in millions)	Prior Year Carryover Funds Available for Programs (in millions)*
Evaluation of the Office of Victims of Crime Wraparound Victim Legal Assistance Network Demonstration Project*****	$3.6	
Office of Justice Programs Assessment for Management and Administration (M&A)	$0.3	
Peer Review of Sexual Assault Forensic Exam Program Applications	$0.1	
Carryover****	$0.0	
SUBTOTAL	$4.0	$0.0
TOTAL	$125.0	$0.6

*   Awards made in FY 2012 with prior year "Carryover" funds.

**   NIJ elects to administer the DNA Backlog Reduction Program through an NIJ-established formula that is detailed annually in the solicitation document. The funds are discretionary in nature (i.e., there is no statutory requirement to administer them as a formula program).

***   DNA funds shown here for the Postconviction DNA Testing Assistance Program are in addition to the $4 million identified in the Appropriations Act for this purpose. An additional $0.1 million was needed to fully fund an application received under the solicitation titled "NIJ FY 2012 Postconviction DNA Testing Assistance Program."

****   NIJ received "no-year" funding for these programs in FY 2012 (funds that did not expire at the end of the fiscal year). "Carryover" funds are those that remained unobligated as of the end of the fiscal year. Depending on the provisions of future appropriations legislation, these funds may be subject to statutory rescission.

***** NIJ transferred these funds via Intra-Agency Reimbursable Agreement to OJP's Office of Victims of Crime, who will oversee this project.

Exhibit 4: Solicitations by Title, Number of Applications and Awards, and Value, FY 2012

Solicitation Title	Applications Received	Awards Made	Value of Awards
1. Applied Research and Development in Forensic Science for Criminal Justice Purposes	168	24	$9,550,515
2. Basic Scientific Research to Support Forensic Science for Criminal Justice Purposes	92	11	$4,964,640
3. Building and Enhancing Researcher-Practitioner Partnerships	53	4	$1,439,800
4. Data Resources Program: Funding for Analysis of Existing Data	37	6	$217,887
5. Desistance From Crime Over the Life Course	24	2	$1,705,164
6. Determining the Relationship between Stress and Unexplained In-Custody Deaths	3	2	$770,690
7. DNA Backlog Reduction Program	117	117	$74,347,305
8. Evaluability Assessment of Law Enforcement Agencies Using the Data-Driven Approaches to Crime and Traffic Safety (DDACTS)	7	1	$299,921
9. Evaluability Assessments of the Circles of Support and Accountability (COSA) Model	5	1	$101,430
10. Evaluating the Impact of the NIJ Body Armor Program	3	1	$399,884
11. Evaluation of the FY 2010 Bureau of Justice Assistance Second Chance Act Adult Offender Reentry Demonstration Projects	28	2	$3,334,022
12. Evaluation of the Implementation of the Sex Offender Treatment Intervention and Progress Scale (SOTIPS)	7	1	$1,496,090
13. Evaluation of the Office for Victims of Crime Wraparound Victim Legal Assistance Network Demonstration Project	1	1	$598,720
14. Evaluation of the Office of Juvenile Justice and Delinquency Prevention FY 2010 Second Chance Act Juvenile Offender Reentry Demonstration Projects	10	1	$1,997,100
15. Longitudinal Data on Teen Dating Violence: Postdoctoral Fellowship	6	2	$496,436
16. Paul Coverdell Forensic Science Improvement Grants Program	196	75	$10,586,098
17. Ph.D. Graduate Research Fellowship Program	66	11	$274,986
18. Postconviction DNA Testing Assistance Program	9	5	$3,546,504
19. Replication Research on Sexual Violence Case Attrition	3	1	$1,197,686
20. Research and Evaluation on Children Exposed to Violence	35	3	$1,553,210
21. Research and Evaluation in Justice Systems	35	3	$1,854,003
22. Research and Evaluation on Metropolitan Crime	8	2	$1,250,127
23. Research and Evaluation on Trafficking in Persons	23	4	$1,462,610
24. Research and Evaluation on Violence Against Women: Sexual Violence, Stalking, and Teen Dating Violence	41	4	$2,489,547

25. Research on Domestic Radicalization	15	6	$3,053,281
26. Research on Illegal Prescription Drug Market Interventions	15	3	$863,209
27. Research on Policing	18	1	$341,469
28. Research on the Impact of Technology on Policing Strategies in the 21st Century	19	1	$999,587
29. Research on the Link Between Victimization and Offending	10	1	$426,181
30. Social Science Research on Indigent Defense	15	3	$1,624,578
31. Solving Cold Cases with DNA	87	22	$7,580,191
32. Testing Geospatial Police Strategies and Exploring their Relationship to Criminological Theories	11	2	$896,977
33. The Impact of Different Safety Equipment Modalities on Reducing Correctional Officer Injuries	2	0	$0
34. Using DNA Technology to Identify the Missing	13	4	$3,194,296
35. Violent Victimization Among Racial and Ethnic Minorities	20	1	$231,203
36. W.E.B. Du Bois Fellowship for Research in Race, Gender, Culture and Crime	11	2	$198,990
	1228	330	$144,344,337

Continuations of Awards Made in Prior Years

Office	Awards Made	Value of Awards
Office of Investigative and Forensic Sciences Continuations	4	$3,649,331
Office of Research and Evaluation Continuations	11	$5,968,285
Office of Science and Technology Continuations	18	$13,656,286
Subtotal	33	$23,273,902
Grand Total	363	$168 million

Exhibit 5: Number of Awards, FY 2008-2012

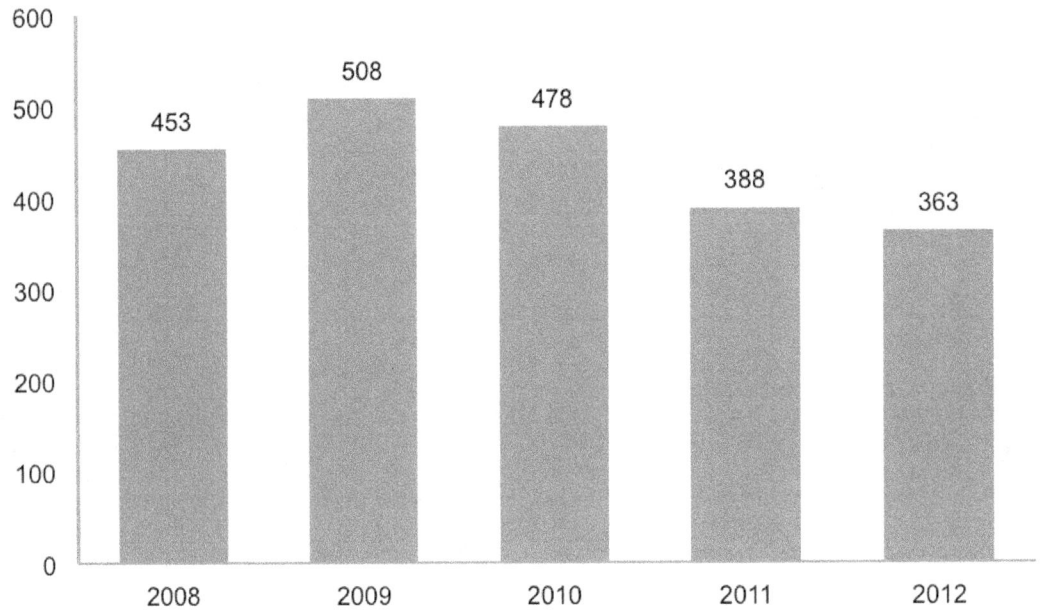